Secrets To Creating The Perfect Speech

How to create a speech that will make your message be remembered forever!

"Practical, proven techniques that will help you to make your next speech a success"

Dr. Jim Anderson

Published by:
Blue Elephant Consulting
Tampa, Florida

Copyright © 2013 by Dr. Jim Anderson

All rights reserved. No part of this book may be reproduced of transmitted in any form or by any means, electronic or mechanical, including photocopying, recording or by any information storage and retrieval system without written permission of the publisher, except for inclusion of brief quotations in a review.

Printed in the United States of America

Library of Congress Control Number: 2013921826

ISBN-13: 978-1494284398
ISBN-10: 1494284391

Warning – Disclaimer

The purpose of this book is to educate and entertain. This book does not promise or guarantee that anyone following the ideas, tips, suggestions, techniques or strategies will be hired. It is the discretion of employers if you will or will not be hired. The author, publisher and distributor(s) shall have neither liability nor responsibility to anyone with respect to any loss or damage caused, or alleged to be caused, directly or indirectly by the information contained in this book.

Other Books By The Author

Product Management

- How To Have A Successful Product Manager Career: The Things That You Need To Be Doing TODAY In Order To Have A Successful Product Manager Career

- Product Manager Product Success: How to keep your product on track and make it become a success

- Communication Skills For Product Managers: The Communication Skills That Product Managers Need To Know How To Use In Order To Have A Successful Product

- Product Failure Lessons For Product Managers: Examples Of Products That Have Failed For Product Managers To Learn From

Public Speaking

- Secrets To Planning The Perfect Speech

- Secrets To Organizing The Perfect Speech: How to organize the best speech of your life!

CIO Skills

- CIO Business Skills: How CIOs can work effectively with the rest of the company!

- Managing Your CIO Career: Steps That CIOs Have To Take In Order To Have A Long And Successful Career

- CIO Communication Skills Secrets: Tips And Techniques For CIOs To Use In Order To Become Better Communicators

IT Manager Skills

- IT Manager Budgeting Skills

- IT Manager Career Secrets: Tips And Techniques That IT Managers Can Use In Order To Have A Successful Career

Negotiating

- Preparing For Your Next Negotiation: What You Need To Do BEFORE A Negotiation Starts In Order To Get The Best Possible Deal

- How To Open Your Next Negotiation: How To Start A Negotiation In Order To Get The Best Possible Outcome

Miscellaneous

- Power Distribution Unit (PDU) Secrets: What Everyone Who Works In A Data Center Needs To Know!

- Making The Jump: How To Land Your Dream Job When You Get Out Of College!

Acknowledgements

Any book like this one is the result of years of real-world work experience. In my over 25 years of working for 7 different firms, I have met countless fantastic people and I've been mentored by some truly exceptional ones. Although I've probably forgotten some of the people who made me the person that I am today, here is my attempt to finally give them the recognition that they so truly deserve:

- Thomas P. Anderson
- Art Puett
- Bobbi Marshall
- Bob Boggs

Dr. Jim Anderson

This book is dedicated to my wife Lori. None of this would have been possible without her love and support.

Thanks for the best 21 years of my life (so far)...!

Table Of Contents

WHAT'S THE BEST WAY GIVE A GREAT SPEECH? 8

ABOUT THE AUTHOR 10

CHAPTER 1: THE THREE KEY GOALS OF ANY PRESENTATION 15

CHAPTER 2: HOW TO CONNECT WITH YOUR AUDIENCE 18

CHAPTER 3: DIFFERENCES COUNT WHEN YOU ARE PRESENTING 21

CHAPTER 4: GET 'EM TO UNDERSTAND, GET 'EM TO REMEMBER 24

CHAPTER 5: HOW TO WRITE A SPEECH 27

CHAPTER 6: QUICK HIT: TOP 10 TIPS TO REMEMBER WHEN WRITING A SPEECH 30

CHAPTER 7: PERSUASIVE SPEECH TIME: HOW TO DEAL WITH UNSPEAKABLE SUBJECTS 33

CHAPTER 8: COMMUNICATION SKILLS FROM THE MASTER: EDWARD TUFTE 36

CHAPTER 9: KILLING TIME UNTIL YOU RUN THE WORLD — HOW TO USE QUOTES IN YOUR NEXT SPEECH 39

CHAPTER 10: DYNAMIC HUMOR: WHAT'S A PUBLIC SPEAKER TO DO? 42

CHAPTER 11: A PUBLIC SPEAKER'S TIPS FOR WRITING A SPEECH 45

CHAPTER 12: 10 TIPS FOR BECOMING A PUBLIC SPEAKER WHO CAN TALK ABOUT MONEY 48

What's The Best Way Give A Great Speech?

There are speeches, and then there are great speeches. As public speakers it's the great speeches that we want to give; however, how is one to go about creating such a speech?

It turns out that creating a great speech really is not all that hard to do if you know how. The first thing that you have to do is to realize that a great speech is one that your audience will enjoy listening to. However, even more important than that is that long after you are done speaking, they are going to remember what you said. A great speech is one that "sticks" with your audience.

Your speech is also going to have to be persuasive. Every speech that we give is given for a reason. We want to change the way that our audience views their world. This means that you are going to have to change their minds. The key to doing that in a great speech is to find a way to be persuasive. Tap into your audience's desire to believe in something and make them believe in you and your ideas.

We can all learn how to transform a plain ordinary speech into a great speech if we know where to look. There are great speakers out there who have tips for us. We can learn how to add humor to our speeches and we can learn how to write better speeches in the first place.

All of these things are possible, you just have to be told how to do them. That's exactly what this book is all about – how to create the perfect speech. We are going to step you through each of the different techniques that you can use to make your next speech unforgettable. Speech perfection is within your grasp!

For more information on what it takes to be a great public speaker, check out my blog, The Accidental Communicator, at:

www.TheAccidentalCommunicator.com

Good luck!

- Dr. Jim Anderson

About The Author

I must confess that I never set out to be a public speaker. When I went to school, I studied Computer Science and thought that I'd get a nice job programming and that would be that. Well, at least part of that plan worked out!

My first job was working for Boeing on their F/A-18 fighter jet program. I spent my days programming fighter jet software in assembly language and I loved it. The U.S. government decided to save some money and went looking for other countries to sell this plane to. This put me into an unfamiliar role: I started to meet with foreign military officials and I ended up having to give speeches in order to explain what my product did.

Time moved on and so did I. I found myself working for Siemens, the big German telecommunications company. They were making phone switches and selling them to the seven U.S. phone companies. The problem was that the switches were too complicated. Customers couldn't tell the difference between one complicated phone switch from another complicated phone switch. Once again I found myself standing in front of the room giving speeches in order to explain what these complicated machines did and why ours were better than anyone else's.

I've spent over 25 years working as a product manager for both big companies and startups. This has given me an opportunity to do many, many presentations for customers, at conferences, and everywhere in-between.

I now live in Tampa Florida where I spend my time managing my consulting business, Blue Elephant Consulting, teaching college courses at the University of South Florida, and traveling to work with companies like yours to share the knowledge that I have about how to create and deliver powerful and effective speeches.

I'm always available to answer questions and I can be reached at:

Dr. Jim Anderson
Blue Elephant Consulting
Email: jim@BlueElephantConsulting.com
Facebook: http://goo.gl/1TVoK
Web: **www.BlueElephantConsulting.com**

"Unforgettable communication skills that will set your ideas free…"

Create Speeches That Motivate Your Audiences And Get Your Message Heard!

Dr. Jim Anderson is available to provide training and coaching on the topics that are the most important to people who have to speak in public: how can I create a speech that people want to hear and how can I deliver in a way that will allow me to connect with my audience and get my point across to them?

Dr. Anderson believes that in order to both learn and remember what he says, speakers need to laugh. Each one of his speeches is full of fun and humor so that what he says "sticks" with everyone.

Dr. Anderson's Public Speaking Training Includes:

1. How to plan your next speech: pick your purpose and understand your audience.
2. What's the best way to get PowerPoint and Keynote to work with you, not against you?
3. What do you need to do when you are presenting in order to truly connect with your audience?

Dr. Jim Anderson presents over 100 speeches per year. To invite Dr. Anderson to speak at your event, contact him at:

Phone: 813-418-6970 or
Email: jim@BlueElephantConsulting.com

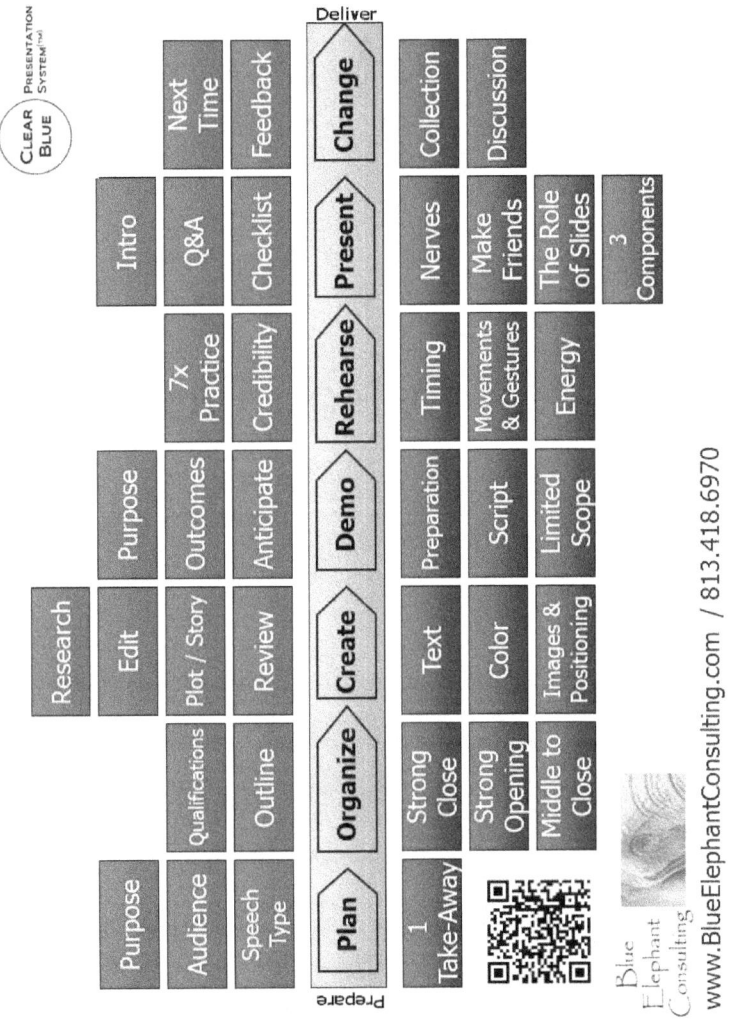

Blue Elephant Consulting has created the **Clear Blue™** presentation system for creating and delivering powerful and memorable presentations. The contents of this book are based on lessons learned during the development of the Clear Blue system. Contact Blue Elephant Consulting to learn more about the Clear Blue presentation system.

Chapter 1

The Three Key Goals Of Any Presentation

Chapter 1: The Three Key Goals Of Any Presentation

Often when we are asked to give a presentation, we spend a great deal of time working on WHAT we want to say. Unfortunately we really should be spending more time on HOW we say it. In order to do a better job of this, it would probably be a good idea if we took a step back and spent just a moment or two thinking about what we'd like to accomplish by making this presentation.

If your goal is to get it over with, well then congrats — you will probably be successful in some fashion. However, if as long as you are going to the effort to prepare and present the info, you'd like to actually make an impact, perhaps even change the world, then it would seem as though you should have some higher goals.

In his book **Clear and to the Point**, Stephen Kosslyn proposes that we have three goals in mind for every presentation:

1. **Connect With Your Audience:** If they can't pick out how your presentation relates to them or their lives, then they just won't care what you are talking about.

2. **Direct and Hold Their Attention**: You need to tell a story that is so compelling that they are hanging on your every word, waiting for your next revelation.

3. **Promote Understanding & Memory**: How you present your information should be easy to understand and done in such a way that when you are done and the slides are put away, your audience can still remember what you said and why it all made sense.

Whew! That doesn't seem so hard now does it? Well, it actually is quite difficult to do well. Use these three simple ways to start to improve your presentations so that you easily accomplish all of your goals.

Chapter 2

How To Connect With Your Audience

Chapter 2: How To Connect With Your Audience

So let's talk turkey: no matter how complex the information that you are trying to communicate is, nor what setting you are trying to communicate it in, just how can you go about getting what you have to say to "stick" in your audience's minds? What can you say or do that is going to get them to talk about it and think about it long after you have completed what you have to say?

There are several things that you have to do and the first is to make sure that you connect with your audience. How to do that is what seems to escape all too many public speakers. Stephen Kosslyn in his book **Clear and to The Point** lays out a number of different ways to do this. Here are two of my favorites:

Your communication, no matter what form it takes, is going to have the greatest impact when you present neither too much nor too little information.

Think about this one for just a moment. It's very simple to understand; however, it's very hard to do correctly. Ultimately I believe that the key here is to start from the end: what do you want them to walk away with? You should then add everything that will be needed to make this happen and take away anything that does not contribute to this goal.

Your communication requires you to have prior knowledge of your audience's pertinent concepts, jargon, and symbols.

In the end, you've got to know your audience. If you present your information in a way that is different from how they communicate, then you are requiring them to work in order to understand what you are trying to say and there is a good chance that they may be unwilling to do this. Assuming that your audience knows more than they do or less than they really do will result in the communication of your material falling on deaf ears. Talk to them in a way that they want to be talked to.

Chapter 3

Differences Count When You Are Presenting

Chapter 3: Differences Count When You Are Presenting

Ok, so you've got a big presentation coming up and you know that you want to make a difference and have the audience walk away with a good understanding of the complex info that you are going to present. What can you do to really make sure that you key points get hammered home?

Setting yourself on fire halfway through the presentation or using trained animals both would be great, if impractical ways to accomplish this. How about two simpler ways that public speakers always seem to forget as we pull together our presentations?

Audience Attention is drawn to LARGE differences that are perceptible.

Let's say that you've got a slide that contains one of the key points that you want to make to your audience. There are probably other things on that slide (like a title?). You need to make sure that your key point, be it a number, a comparison, a figure, etc. jumps out at your audience.

Background images, scrolling text, clipart, video clips, etc. are all swell; however, if they distract from your key point then they need to go away. Keep in mind that PowerPoint's ability to have items join the slide via animation might be a good way to lead up to and introduce the key point.

People group elements into units automatically, which they then remember

The human mind is an amazing thing. We can quickly take in large quantities of information and rapidly make decisions about it. You can make this talent work for or against you in a presentation.

Things that you place close to each other on a slide will automatically be considered to be related by your audience. A good example of this is labels and the thing that they are labeling. A bad example of this would be a graph that shows that both the price of copper ore and the price of apples have both increased by 25% in the past 6 months.

Both items would be shown closely together on the same graph and the audience would associate them. However, they really have nothing to do with each other (unless you are trying to talk about the cost of copper apples…).

Just a few things to consider when you are making that last pass though the big presentation that you've created — do your main points jump out or are they buried?

Chapter 4

Get 'Em To Understand, Get 'Em To Remember

Chapter 4: Get 'Em To Understand, Get 'Em To Remember

Sigh, so you've spent all that time collecting your information, writing the report, making the slides and even created a great handout. Now how much of your presentation do you really think that your audience will remember 30 minutes after you are done, 1 hour later, 1 day later, how about at the end of a month?

Getting our information to first be understood by our audience is one way to be a successful communicator. The other skill that you must have is finding a way to get your message(s) to stick in your audience's memory.

To promote understanding of your message, remember that people DO judge a book by its cover. In presentations this means that your audience will assume that if you have more of something in a figure, then the quantity of that thing is greater.

Think about if you were trying to present plans for a new airplane and were trying to communicate how far it could fly. If you decided to show this by using circles that showed how much fuel was required to fly a given distance. The circle for existing planes would be larger than the circle for your new plane. Although you are trying to communicate that your new plane can fly further, your figure is making it hard for your audience to understand this point.

We communicate information by changing things. As we move from one diagram or graph to the next if we've changed something, then our audience expects that that change really means something and we're trying to tell them something.

This also means that if you want to communicate to your audience that there is a change in meaning, then you must make a change in the appearance of your figure / graph.

Ok, last point to be made: just like this book chapter, everyone has a limit to the amount of new information that they can take in. If you overload them with information, then they will not understand the message that you are trying to communicate. If you have a lot of information to present, then you can communicate it if, and only if, you present it piece by piece so that your audience can absorb it little by little.

Chapter 5

How To Write A Speech

Chapter 5: How To Write A Speech

I was asked to give a speech for a local company's "high achievers" group a little while back. It had been quite some time since I had actually had to sit down and think long and hard about what message I really wanted to get across to an audience. This made me go do some research on how good speechwriters find ideas that really shine.

Everyone who writes speeches for a living seems to agree about one thing: just get the first draft done. There are countless stories about folks who get hung up on trying to write the perfect speech and who spend so much time editing word after word that they never complete the speech. Just let the words flow and resist the urge to edit. Once it's all out there, then you can go back and have at it.

Write for the ear not the eye. What sounds great on paper probably sounds stilted and awkward when read aloud. For example, we use a lot of contractions when we speak (can't, won't, shouldn't) but we don't use them as much when we write. This difference will show up as a wordy, formal tone in any speech. Solve this problem by reading your speech out loud and actually listening to how it sounds. Then go back and rewrite, rewrite, rewrite.

PowerPoint is not all bad. Dr. John Medina's book **Brain Rules** discusses how audiences lose focus after 10 minutes, so shifting gears, telling a story, etc. every 10 minutes will keep them focused and awake.

Another rule is that a combination of both auditory and visual stimuli make your message 6 times more memorable than auditory alone. What this means is that if you use it the way that it should be used (as a helper, not a crutch), PowerPoint can boost the impact of your speech. But be careful — it's easy to go overboard. My favorite saying is "There is a reason that you never see PowerPoint used during a eulogy."

Writing a speech should be an adventure. Often where we think that the effort will take us ends up not being where we finally arrive. However, doing a good job of speech writing will pay dividends that will have a value that lasts long after the speech is done.

Chapter 6

Quick Hit: Top 10 Tips To Remember When Writing A Speech

Chapter 6: Quick Hit: Top 10 Tips To Remember When Writing A Speech

You might think that you have the most amazing information to share with your audience; however, if you don't structure your speech correctly, your message will never "stick" with them. You need to have a strong opening and closing in order to get your message across. Here are 10 tips to keep in mind when you finally get around to sitting down and writing that killer speech to end all speeches:

1. Be sure to plan and practice the opening and closing parts of your speech just as much as you do the middle of the speech.

2. Provide closure for your audience by re-using the same words that you used in your opening in your closing. This will show everyone how you've brought things together.

3. Never, ever, ever apologize or complain. The audience should be thankful that you took the time to talk to them.

4. Don't use definitions for terms that have clearly been lifted out of a dictionary. This will seem forced and will break any connection that you've established with your audience.

5. Don't assume that your audience knows anything about what you are talking about. Skip the subject specific acronyms and jargon. I always like to assume that my Mom's sitting in the audience and I write my speech for her to understand what I'm talking about.

6. Don't be a dork and say things like "This is the end of my speech". Note that saying "In conclusion…" is just as bad.

7. Don't introduce new material as a part of your closing. The closing is there to allow you to wrap things up — not to launch a new speech.

8. In your conclusion, don't suddenly change topics. If you were speaking about the need to get a college education, don't wrap up by saying that high school is where we learn life's most important lessons.

9. Never abandon the podium. Wait for the meeting leader or the MC to come out and take control. If you just walk away, everyone will be confused as to what comes next.

10. Always make yourself available after the speech to answer questions and greet people. This is not for you to feel good, but rather it is for some of your audience to get closure on what you said.

This list is by no means complete, but it sure can provide a great start that will allow you to write a speech that is better than any other speech out there!

Chapter 7

Persuasive Speech Time: How To Deal With Unspeakable Subjects

Chapter 7: Persuasive Speech Time: How To Deal With Unspeakable Subjects

In the world of public speaking, we actually have it pretty good. We generally don't work around spinning industrial machinery nor do we operate fork-lifts or work out in the hot sun. More or less everyone remains fairly healthy and we generally don't get injured on the job.

That being said, we do live in the real world and bad things happen to people. When something bad happens to a member of your team or your department, communicating with the rest of the team about what is going on is a critical part of your job.

As always, the lawyers often jump in with valid concerns about the revealing of other people's personal information, etc. Let's put that aside for right now and make an abstract concept more concrete: let's talk about how you would handle it if a member of your department died.

If it falls on your shoulders to let everyone know what's going on, then this topic will require more tact, knowledge, and preparation than just about any other discussion you will have. Do it correctly and you'll be viewed as a sensitive person. Do it poorly, and you'll instantly lose the respect of your team.

News of this kind of shocking nature will generate the full range of emotions in your audience. This, somewhat amazingly, includes hostility. The loss of a teammate could cause someone to get angry about having to pick up their work when they feel that they are already overloaded.

This may not be a real issue, but instead it is how they start to deal with the loss. This will be the wrong time for you to get into a fight with someone as they are trying to come to terms with what you are saying. Instead, stay professional no matter what and make sure that you stay tuned in to your audience. One way to stay tuned in with your audience is to be sure to maintain eye contact with them. This shows them that you are talking "to them", not "at them".

It's the small details that will get remembered. Hopefully it goes without saying that your body language will always be talking louder than your mouth in this case.

When you are talking about grief, you need to be sure to choose your words very carefully. In the case of a teammate's death, saying over and over again that he's "dead" or "been killed" can be very harsh and jarring. Saying it differently and talking about the "loss" can communicate the same meaning in a more gentle way.

Finally, in our multicultural workplace, make sure that you have names correct. Nothing could be more disrespectful than a verbal fumble at this point in time.

We're lucky because we seem to be able to avoid having to deal with "heavy" topics most of the time. However, when these situations come up, and they always do, being ready to say the right things in the right way can make all the difference in the world.

Chapter 8

Communication Skills From The Master: Edward Tufte

Chapter 8: Communication Skills From The Master: Edward Tufte

If you don't know who Edward Tufte is, then you really should. He is a Professor Emeritus at Yale University and his specialty is teaching people how to present data using information graphics. He is truly an expert on the best way to present complex information.

A long time I was scanning the web when I ran across some notes that Craig Kaplan up at the University of Waterloo had jotted down on how to deliver great presentations after attending one of Tufte's seminars. I now share these suggestions on how to give a good presentation with the reverence that one must show to the words of someone who is really, really good at what they do:

- **Show Up Early!**: Good things happen to those who show up early. Specifically, you can solve problems before they become unsolvable and you can take the time to introduce yourself to the audience as they arrive. This way when you start to speak neither one of you will be a stranger.

- **Have A Strong Opening**: There are three questions that every opening must quickly answer: (1) What's the problem?, (2) Who cares?, and (3) What's your solution? Answer these questions and the audience will listen to your every word.

- **PGP**: As you introduce a new sub-topic, make sure that you move from the **P**articular, to the **G**eneral, and then back to the **P**articular. Although what you want the audience to take away from your presentation is the general info, the particulars will help make the info "stick".

- **Know Your Audience** — By What They Read!: This is Tufte's twist on an old maxim of public speaking. He believes that knowing what your audience reads will help you understand what styles of information presentation works best for them.

- **Take Care When Answering Questions**: There is a good possibility that your audience's take-away impression of your presentation won't be based on your presentation, but rather on how you answer questions AFTER the presentation. Allow for long pauses after the question has been asked and before you answer — this will give more weight to your reply.

- **Let Everyone Know That You Believe In Your Material**: Speak with lots of conviction! Clearly letting everyone know that you believe in everything that you are telling them is the key to getting them to believe it just as much as you do.

There you have it. Now please remember that Tufte also has the ability to use amazing graphics with his presentations that clearly communicate what lots of data has to say. However, even the best graphics won't do you any good if you don't remember these presentation rules from the master.

Chapter 9

Killing Time Until YOU Run The World — How To Use Quotes In Your Next Speech

Chapter 9: Killing Time Until YOU Run The World — How To Use Quotes In Your Next Speech

Man, once you are in charge, things are going to be different around here! Specifically, you won't have to work so hard to convince your audience that they should see things your way.

However, until that day arrives, perhaps it would be worth our time to take a look at a few ways to persuade your audience to come over to your way of thinking. We've already discussed the power of keeping your focus tightly centered on a few key issues that matter to your audience and then drawing them in using stories. That's a good way to start, but there is much more that you can do...

Although you may be a well-respected person to your audience and you might even be the world's leading expert on whatever topic you are talking about, unfortunately that might not be enough. For whatever reason, a portion of your audience has probably already made up their mind to not agree with you.

Your biggest challenge is going to be to win them over to your side. One powerful tool that you have available to you is the quote. It took me a long time to understand why presenters used quotes – to me they just seemed like so much fancy window dressing.

It turns out that I was wrong. A quote is a very powerful tool. What happens when a presenter uses a quote is that they are almost magically summoning the person who originally spoke those words to stand beside the speaker and say the words once again.

By referencing someone else's words, it will leave the impression with your audience that if that person were present in the room with you, they would approve of what you are currently saying.

If you are talking about **raising** taxes and you use a quote from Ronald Reagan to support your case, then that would probably be too much of a stretch for most people to make. However, if you were talking about helping clashing groups to find common ground and you used a quote from Nelson Mandela then it would be a powerful way to reinforce your position.

A fantastic fact about our human brains that sales people have known for a long time is that if our brain can verify that two things are true, then it will accept a third thing as being true also. The formal name for this technique is called "Pacing and Leading".

What this means for you as a presenter is that with a little careful preparation, you can design your presentation to help you persuade your audience that you are correct. As an example, if you start out your presentation by saying "Hello, I am John Smith and I work in the IT department." and then follow this up with "I'm going to explain to you why an Oracle database is the correct product to use on our next project."

Keep in mind that you cannot use this technique to say something that is clearly untrue. Your third point must be a reasonable conclusion.

There you have it – two more powerful techniques to leave your audience cheering for your way of looking at the world. Used correctly, you can use your words to do your work for you – and isn't that what communicating is all about?

Chapter 10

Dynamic Humor: What's A Public Speaker To Do?

Chapter 10: Dynamic Humor: What's A Public Speaker To Do?

In real estate, they say that the value of a property is based on location, location, location. In speaking, you can divide your speech up into three separate parts: the opening, the body, and the closing. I firmly believe that the value of your speech is all about the opening, opening, opening.

Studies have shown that you have everyone's attention when you are starting your speech. As more words tumble out of your mouth, you will lose more and more of your audience as they start to tap on their iPhones, talk with the neighbor, or boot up their laptop. How can you connect with your audience right off the bat – and hold their attention for your entire speech? One word: humor.

Perhaps this is a good time for me to be very, very clear: I'm not talking about "classic jokes" – you know the type that begins "Two men walk into a bar and…". Instead, the kind of humor that I'm referring to probably better called off-the-cuff humor. The most dangerous kind of humor!

Why take the risk of using dynamic humor? Simple, the payoffs are so great that it's well worth the risk. The key is to identify where you are going to get your raw material for your dynamic humor.

What you need to do is before your speech starts, you need to place yourself in your audience's position. What are they feeling? Is the room hot or cold? Is there a distracting noise? What did the previous speaker say – did he say something shocking or controversial? Don't forget food, if breakfast or break snacks have been served then how did that go?

By realizing what your audience has experienced, you can do one of three different things:

- Create an analogy
- Take things to an extreme
- Make a word association

Another source of great dynamic humor material is to take a look at the demographics of your audience: is it all women, all men, young, old, Northerners? Finally, take a careful look at the agenda for the event. If you've been asked to talk about next year's business cases and the person who comes after you will be talking about budget cutbacks for next year, then you've got to comment on this!

Chapter 11

A Public Speaker's Tips For Writing A Speech

Chapter 11: A Public Speaker's Tips For Writing A Speech

Go to any book store and you'll find a 6" long section of books that promise to teach you how to deliver a speech in public better. What's all too often missing from this avalanche of advice is any real guidance on how to create a speech that will work for your audience.

No matter how well you deliver a speech, it will all be for naught if the speech itself does not do a good job of telling your story & making your point.

Perhaps this is a good time for us to take a moment and consider what a speech really is (I'm a big fan of the basics). At its core, a speech is simply an opportunity for you to tell your audience about something that you are interested in.

The part that all too many people seem to overlook is that you really want your speech to be **memorable**. In other words, after you stop talking, you would like people in the audience to be able to remember what you said, and even better, take action based on it.

This all means that WHAT you say and HOW you say it are very important. Here's the zinger: it's not the topic that is boring, but rather how it's presented that can be boring.

Sometimes you get to pick what you want to talk about, most of the time you are told. The very first question that you need to ask yourself is: why am I giving this speech? What is my one, single purpose?

This can generally be found in one of five big words: to inform, to inspire, to entertain, to motivate, or to convince. Once you've picked one of these (yes, you can only pick one) then you are set to do the most important part of speech creation: pick the slant.

The slant (or focus if you prefer) is what makes your speech stand out. You want to pick a particular angle that your audience may not be expecting and then you approach your subject from there.

Finally, you need to boil your entire speech down into one single sentence. This sentence, if printed on cards and handed out to your audience, would leave them with the essence of your speech if you were not able to show up and speak.

You would never hand out this sentence and in fact you might not even use it as part of your speech. However, simply by creating it you will have allowed the main point of your speech to crystallize in your head that that will make all the difference in the world.

Chapter 12

10 Tips For Becoming A Public Speaker Who Can Talk About Money

Chapter 12: 10 Tips For Becoming A Public Speaker Who Can Talk About Money

Money – it's a love / hate thing. We all would like to have lots of the stuff; however, most people (us included) would probably rather lose a finger than have to sit though yet another incredibly boring presentation about the green stuff. Why is this?

It's actually pretty easy to understand what's wrong with most presentations about money: it is presented in a boring way, the PowerPoint slides that are used are crammed with numbers that are way too small for any human to be able to read, and the presenter often uses vocabulary that we don't understand. What can be done to fix this?

We already know that one of the most effective ways to deliver a presentation that will "stick" with your audience is to tell them a compelling story. A presentation about money should be no different – it's the story that you tell that will get your point across. Keeping that in mind, here are some tips that will make your next presentation on money unforgettable:

1. **K.I.S.S:** No, not the rock group, but rather **K**eep **I**t **S**imple **S**tupid. In other words, whenever you talk about money there can be the tendency to say too much. DON'T DO IT! Instead, before you create your speech write out a single sentence that contains the message that you want your audience to walk away with. Then, when you are describing some financial tool re-read this sentence and determine if what you are talking about supports it. If not, then drop it and move on.

2. **Come Early, Leave Late:** This is just a basic speaker tip; however, it's even more important when you are talking about money. Making sure that you don't have to worry

about your equipment or the room gives you more time to focus on what you are going to be saying. Not having to run out at the end means that you can provide more detail for those who really want it.

3. **Bring A Partner To Help – Mr. Handout:** Since much of what you may be talking about can be (a) complex and (b) detailed, this is one speech that you do want to provide a handout for. However, don't do what too many speakers do and just give everyone a copy of your slides. Instead, create a special handout that provides detailed information about things that you didn't have time to cover.

4. **Careful About Colors:** Since so much of what is shown in any presentation on money is charts, you need to carefully check your colors. Stay away from the common color-blindness colors and make sure that all of your text is readable from the back of the room.

5. **Shut Her Down When You Don't Need Her:** All too often an audience in a talk about money can start to pay more attention to the slides than the speaker. One way to put a stop to this is to either turn off the projector every so often or, even better yet, put a completely black slide into your deck when you want all eyes on you. It's startling and it works really well.

6. **Do The Dark / Light Thing:** Making your PowerPoint slides readable is critical. One way to help this happen is to make sure that the contrast between your slides' background color and the foreground colors is very distinct. For a large room, I've found that making your slide background dark while making your text and drawings light colored makes everything readable even from the back of the room.

7. **Turn Off The Hollywood Effects:** PowerPoint and other presentation applications allow you to go wild on how one slide goes away and the next one shows up – transitions. Here's a suggestion: don't. Either pick one transition and use it throughout your presentation or only vary the transition when you really want to draw attention to the new slide. Otherwise you risk training your audience to look forward to your next transition and not what you are saying.

8. **Don't Create A Fighter Pilot Eye Exam:** I can't tell you just how important this one is – make sure that you keep your font selections to a minimum and make sure that all text is large enough to be read. I like to choose "sans serf" fonts because they don't have the loopy stuff and are generally easier to read. I've also found that the 18 pt font size is the smallest that you want to use, otherwise it just gets too hard to read.

9. **Remember What A Picture Is Worth:** Instead of trying to overwhelm your audience with words that describe technical financial terms, try to use more charts and graphs. Displaying a chart and then talking about it gives your audience time to apply your words to real situations and promotes understanding and retention.

10. **Remember That Only 5 lbs. Will Fit In A 5 lbs. Bag:** Avoid the #1 sin of public speakers who talk about money – putting too much information on a single slide. We can fall in love with the way that we describe something and we like to add more and more details to it. However, take a moment and think about your poor audience. Try to present just the bare minimum amount of information that they need on each slide.

By following these simple tips you can create a powerful presentation that makes an impression on your audience and leaves them with the thoughts and ideas that you want them to have.

It's from the forge of failure that the steel of success is formed.

Hard Work Does Not Guarantee Success, But Success Does Not Happen Without Hard Work.

- Dr. Jim Anderson

Create Speeches That Motivate Your Audiences And Get Your Message Heard!

Dr. Jim Anderson is available to provide training and coaching on the topics that are the most important to people who have to speak in public: how can I create a speech that people want to hear and how can I deliver in a way that will allow me to connect with my audience and get my point across to them?

Dr. Anderson believes that in order to both learn and remember what he says, speakers need to laugh. Each one of his speeches is full of fun and humor so that what he says "sticks" with everyone.

Dr. Anderson's Public Speaking Training Includes:

1. How to plan your next speech: pick your purpose and understand your audience.
2. What's the best way to get PowerPoint and Keynote to work with you, not against you?
3. What do you need to do when you are presenting in order to truly connect with your audience?

Dr. Jim Anderson presents over 100 speeches per year. To invite Dr. Anderson to speak at your event, contact him at: **Phone: 813-418-6970** or **Email: jim@BlueElephantConsulting.com**

Photo Credits:

Cover - By: Denise Krebs
http://www.flickr.com/photos/mrsdkrebs/

Chapter 1 - By: Donovan Beeson
http://www.flickr.com/photos/donovan_beeson/

Chapter 2 - By: Mr. Moon
http://www.flickr.com/photos/bmune/

Chapter 3 - By: Bert Kaufmann
http://www.flickr.com/photos/22746515@N02/

Chapter 4 - By: Roger Price
http://www.flickr.com/photos/rwp-roger/

Chapter 5 - By: jeffrey james pacres
http://www.flickr.com/photos/jjpacres/

Chapter 6 - By: Sam Churchill
http://www.flickr.com/photos/samchurchill/

Chapter 7 - By: Ed Ng
http://www.flickr.com/photos/subtleness/

Chapter 8 - By: Playing Futures: Applied Nomadology
http://www.flickr.com/photos/centralasian/

Chapter 9 - By: The Author

Chapter 10 - By: Joming
http://www.flickr.com/photos/joming/

Chapter 11 - By: jose angel
http://www.flickr.com/photos/josangel_ap/

Chapter 12 - By: epSos .de
http://www.flickr.com/photos/epsos/

"Secrets To Creating The Perfect Speech"

This book has been written with one goal in mind – to show you how you can create a great speech. We're going to show you what you need to do in order to make your next speech both persuasive and remembered!

Let's Make Your Next Speech A Success!

What You'll Find Inside:

- **THE THREE KEY GOALS OF ANY PRESENTATION**

- **HOW TO CONNECT WITH YOUR AUDIENCE**

- **GET 'EM TO UNDERSTAND, GET 'EM TO REMEMBER**

- **QUICK HIT: TOP 10 TIPS TO REMEMBER WHEN WRITING A SPEECH**

Dr. Jim Anderson brings his 25 years of real-world experience to this book. He's delivered speeches at some of the world's largest firms as well as at many conferences. He's going to show you what you need to do in order to make your next speech a success!

www.ingramcontent.com/pod-product-compliance
Lightning Source LLC
Chambersburg PA
CBHW071819170526
45167CB00003B/1369